# Do You Really Want a Snake?

Bridget Heos • Illustrated by Katya Longhi

Amicus Illustrated is published by Amicus
P.O. Box 1329, Mankato, MN 56002
www.amicuspublishing.us

Library of Congress Cataloging-in-Publication Data
Heos, Bridget, author.
 Do you really want a snake? / by Bridget Heos ; Illustrated by Katya Longhi.
    pages cm. — (Do you really want a pet?)
 Summary: "Several snakes (and the narrator) teach a young boy the
responsibility—and the joys—of caring for a pet snake. Includes "Is this pet
right for me?" quiz"— Provided by publisher.
 Audience: K to grade 3.
 Includes bibliographical references.
 ISBN 978-1-60753-751-9 (library binding) — ISBN 978-1-60753-850-9 (ebook)
1. Snakes as pets–Juvenile literature. 2. Pets–Juvenile literature. I. Longhi, Katya,
illustrator. II. Title. III. Series: Heos, Bridget. Do you really want a pet?
 SF459.S5H46 2015
 639.3'96–dc23                            2014033274

Editor       Rebecca Glaser
Designer     Kathleen Petelinsek

Printed in the United States of America at
Corporate Graphics in North Mankato, Minnesota.

10 9 8 7 6 5 4 3 2 1

# About the Author

Bridget Heos is the author of more than
70 books for children including *Mustache Baby*
and *Mustache Baby Meets His Match*. Her family
has two pets, an old dog named Ben and a young
cat named Homer. You can find out more about
her at www.authorbridgetheos.com.

# About the Illustrator

Katya Longhi was born in southern Italy.
She studied illustration at the Nemo NT
Academy of Digital Arts in Florence. She loves
to create dream worlds with horses, flying
dogs, and princesses in her illustrations.
She currently lives in northern Italy
with her Prince Charming.

So you say you want a snake. You really want a snake. **But do you *really* want a snake?** You'll need a terrarium, which is like an aquarium without water.

Without one . . .

. . . the snake will make your whole house its terrarium.

Or maybe even your whole neighborhood!

HIDEY HOLE

BRANCH

ROCK

Before your snake moves in, cover the bottom of the terrarium with newspapers or wood shavings for bedding.

Add a branch for climbing and a rock. Your snake will rub against the rock to help it shed its skin. Your snake will also need a place to hide and a sturdy water bowl.

But something is missing . . .

. . . a heat lamp! In nature, snakes need the sun to stay warm. The heat lamp will take the place of the sun.

Place the heat lamp over one side of the terrarium. That way, the snake can warm up on one side and cool down on the other. Of course, you'll also need to feed your snake. And snake food is unfortunately . . .

. . . kind of cute. All snakes eat live animals. Garter snakes and other small snakes eat earthworms and guppies.

Bigger snakes eat bigger animals. King snakes, milk snakes, and corn snakes eat mice. In the wild, snakes eat live animals, but in a small space like a terrarium . . .

corn snake

milk snake

king snake

. . . the mouse may fight back. It can actually bite the snake. So it's best to feed pet snakes dead mice. You can buy them at the pet store. Thaw them before feeding your snake.

Unlike most pets, snakes do not eat every day.
Snakes eat about once a week.

You'll also need to clean the cage once a week.
## If you don't . . .

# . . . it will stink!

Change the bedding and scrub the water bowl. Wash your hands after cleaning the cage or touching your snake. Like all reptiles, snakes have bacteria on their skin.

Even with proper care, a snake can get sick.

If your snake is overly tired, has stopped eating, or has blood in its mouth, take it to the vet. You'll need a vet that knows about reptiles.

REPTILE VET

All better? How about some play time with your new pet? Snakes like being alone, but you can hold your pet once or twice a week.

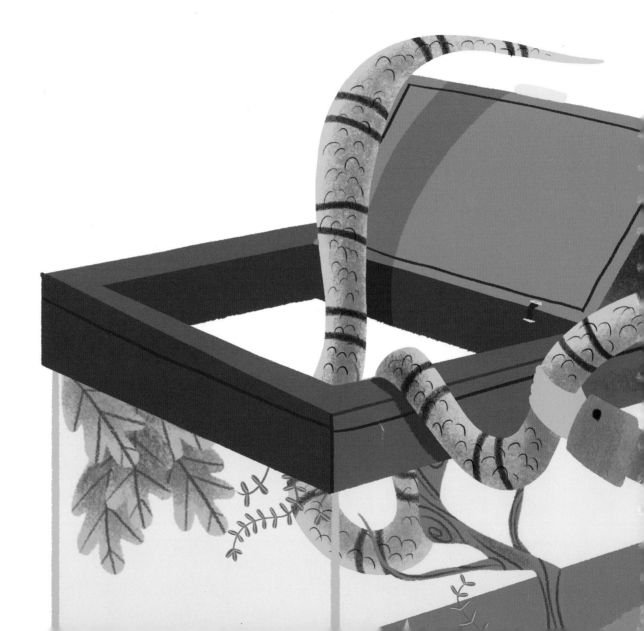

To pick it up, slide one hand under the middle of its body. Don't touch its head. Slide your other hand under its body farther down.

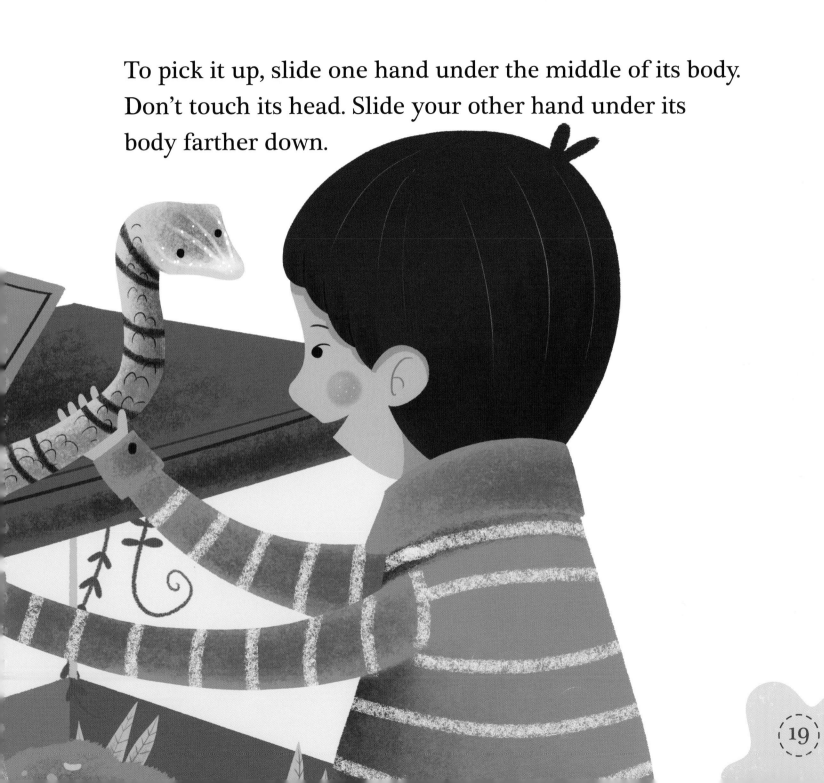

Let the snake slither
over your hands.
Watch how it moves
forward by bending its
body. Aww, that's cute.

So if you're willing to feed, water, and provide a good, clean habitat for your pet, then maybe you really do want a snake.

Now I have a question for the snake. You say you want a person. You really, really want a person.

## But do you *really* want a person?

# QUIZ

## Is this the right pet for me?

Should you get a pet snake? Complete this quiz to find out. (Be sure to talk to breeders, rescue groups, or pet store workers, too!)

1. Are you okay with feeding other animals to your pet?
2. Would you like an animal that is scaly and cool instead of furry and cuddly?
3. Would you like to have a pet that stays in a terrarium most the time?

## If you answered . . .

a. NO TO ONE, you might consider a turtle that eats plants instead.
b. NO TO TWO, a furry animal, like a guinea pig or rabbit, might be better.
c. NO TO THREE, then choose a pet that lives outside a cage, such as a cat or dog.
d. YES TO ALL THREE QUESTIONS, a snake might be the right pet for you!

# Websites

**Corn Snake Care Advice**
*www.petsathome.com/shop/en/pets/corn-snake-advice*
Read about whether a corn snake is the right pet for you, how to set up its terrarium, and how to care for corn snakes.

**Garter Snake Care Guide**
*www.reptilesncritters.com/care-guide-garter-snake.php*
Read all about how to care for garter snakes and other reptiles.

**King Snake, Milk Snake, and Corn Snake**
*www.mypetsmart.com/care-guides/reptile/kingsnake-milksnake-corn-snake/setup-steps.shtml*
Read about how to set up a terrarium for larger breeds of snakes.

**Reptile Care for Beginners**
*www.reptilesmagazine.com/Reptile-Care-For-Beginners/*
Reptiles Magazine offers articles about reptile pet care, choosing a reptile pet, and information for kids who are getting a snake for the first time.

Every effort has been made to ensure that these websites are appropriate for children. However, because of the nature of the Internet, it is impossible to guarantee that these sites will remain active indefinitely or that their contents will not be altered.

# Read More

Armentrout, David and Patricia. *Slithering Snakes and How to Care for Them*. Vero Beach, FL: Rourke Publishing, 2011.

Craats, Rennay. *My Pet Snake*. New York: Weigl, 2011.

Hernandez-Divers, Sonia. *Snakes*. Chicago: Heinemann Library, 2010.

Thomas, Isabel. *Slinky's Guide to Caring for Your Snake*. Chicago: Capstone Heinemann Library, 2015.

Hiss!
Hiss!